Easy-to-Make Decorative Boxes and Desk Accessories

Easy-to-Make Decorative Boxes and Desk Accessories

73 Projects Using Printed Papers and Fabrics

ANNETTE HOLLANDER

*Text prepared by
Maureen Hollander*

*Black and white photographs by
Charles S. Koch and Richard Suavez*

DOVER PUBLICATIONS, INC., NEW YORK

TO TILLIE AND ED

Published in Canada by General Publishing Company, Ltd.,
30 Lesmill Road, Don Mills, Toronto, Ontario.
Published in the United Kingdom by Constable and Company,
Ltd., 10 Orange Street, London WC2H 7EG.

This Dover edition, first published in 1986, is a revised re-
publication of the work originally published by Van Nostrand
Reinhold Company, New York, in 1974 under the title *Bookcraft:
How to Construct Note Pad Covers, Boxes, and Other Useful
Items*. The color photographs that appeared at the front of the
original edition appear in color on the covers of this edition, and
the captions that accompanied the color photographs in the
earlier edition are here gathered at the back of this book in the
"Notes on the Cover Illustrations" section. Omitted from the
present edition are the "Suggested Techniques" and "Selected
Sources of Supplies" sections. A new, updated "Further Reading"
section has been prepared by the author specially for the Dover
edition.

Manufactured in the United States of America
Dover Publications, Inc., 31 East 2nd Street, Mineola, N.Y.
11501

Library of Congress Cataloging-in-Publication Data

Hollander, Annette.
   Easy-to-make decorative boxes and desk accessories.

   Reprint. Originally published: Bookcraft. New York : Van
Nostrand Reinhold Co., c1974.
   Bibliography: p.
   1. Handicraft. 2. Bookbinding. I. Hollander, Maureen. II. Ti-
tle.
TT157.H547   1986   745.593   86-8841
ISBN 0-486-25183-7 (pbk.)

Contents

Preface

I have a memory of my father at Christmas-time, lovingly stooping and gathering together scraps of wrapping paper, gold-glittered, red, and green, that had been torn off anxiously anticipated gifts only minutes before. He smoothed them out with his big hands always hoping to reuse them on another occasion. I know that he considered it a waste to discard these expensive papers after such short and frivolous use. Couldn't something more durable and permanent be made from them?

Most of us have had this feeling when we have found a particularly beautiful paper or fabric. Annette Hollander has given us some unique and personal answers in this new book. She has shared years of experimentation working with cardboard, glue, and paper, imaginatively transforming everyday objects as well as creating new ones. Taking a telephone message or making a mundane shopping list becomes much more pleasurable with Annette's delightful pads and pencils.

Annette has searched all over the world for durable and beautiful papers and fabrics in order to create a unique and very personal object. In her first book, *Decorative Papers and Fabrics,* she has shown many of her own techniques for creating one of a kind papers and fabrics. In this book she develops and fully illustrates ideas for using them. With personal care for every small detail, and consummate and patient craftsmanship, Annette has imaginatively worked out many technical problems that add up to clear and simple solutions. The results are elegant, precise, and beautiful objects.

Annette is a wife and mother of six children. She has created and runs a unique bookcraft business that now includes customers all over the United States and Canada. She has taught widely in Connecticut and given many demonstrations, and the popularity of her classes and enthusiasm of her students is felt by anyone who has worked with her. Craftsmen, artists, teachers, and anyone excited by color, fabric, and pattern can look forward to many hours of creative experimentation with this new book.

Eva Orsini
Artist-craftsman and teacher

Introduction

This is a book of ideas for making booklets, boxes, and other accessories for office and home, using cardboard and covering it with decorative papers and fabrics. Whether you design your own papers and fabrics or use the products of others, this book offers you limitless possibilities for putting them to practical use. Not only are the results handsome in appearance but delightfully satisfying to make. The tools and materials needed for this craft are both inexpensive and readily available.

The methods for constructing the items shown in this book were derived from the two basic techniques of traditional bookbinding: binding a book, and making a slipcase or box for a bound book. But the methods presented here are simplified and require no expensive equipment or time-consuming procedures.

The booklets shown in chapter 2–5 are, for the most part, great simplifications of traditional bookbinding. Since they are suitable for construction by children as well as adults, detailed instructions for making them are given in the text. Chapter 6 presents a simplified version of traditional bookbinding that requires a little more skill and accuracy than the techniques discussed in earlier chapters.

The chapters dealing with the construction of boxes contain detailed instructions only for making each of the two varieties of boxes. Samples of more complex versions of these boxes are shown with diagrams illustrating details of their construction. You are invited to experiment with constructing these boxes in order to discover the wide variety of techniques possible. It is hoped that this will lead you to invent your own constructions, for most of the joy in working with these materials lies in discovering new and interesting ways to create decorative objects.

There are ten Basic Techniques involved in making and covering the cardboard constructions shown in this book. Although they do not necessarily appear in order of difficulty, there is a certain logic to their sequence. Each is numbered and appears in the book before the project that first uses it. Most of these Basic Techniques require familiarity with the previously presented Basic Techniques.

For example, if you want to bind a book as illustrated in Chapter 6, you will need to look back to Basic Technique #1 to find out how to cover cardboard with decorative material. References to previous Basic Techniques are often included in directions for constructing the examples illustrated. But since Basic Techniques occur with great frequency, reference to them is sometimes dropped after the chapter in which they first occur.

Since it is assumed that the reader will proceed through the book in the order in which it is presented, making two or three small items from each chapter before proceeding to the next, the most detailed instructions are given in the earlier chapters. If you wish to begin by constructing an item in one of the later chapters, be sure to read through the Basic Techniques described in the earlier chapters, and practice their applications on scrap material. Several projects are outlined in these chapters, with sample dimensions given.

1. Basic Materials and Their Use

The materials and tools discussed below are used in creating the samples shown in this book. Many hints are offered here for working with these materials and tools. Until you are quite familiar with their use, refer to this section before beginning each item you want to make.

Decorative Papers

Any type of paper may be used to cover items like those shown in this book. Paper with short fibers, such as construction paper, tears easily and should be avoided at points of wear or stress. The papers shown in the examples photographed include both purchased papers, and papers decorated by hand, using techniques such as marbling, batik, and block printing.

If you are interested in learning how to make your own decorative papers (or fabrics), please refer to the list on page 93 of this book for appropriate reading material.

Bookcloth

Commercial bookcloth (and decorative papers) may be obtained from bookcraft- and library-supply outlets. Any other fabric may be used in the same way as bookcloth, but it will be easier to handle and less likely to become soaked with glue if it is lined with paper. To laminate cloth to paper, spread a thin layer of white glue on a piece of newsprint or thin white paper and smooth the paper onto the cloth. When the glue is dry, the fabric may be cut to size. If you are using fabric that has not been laminated, never apply glue directly to the fabric; apply the glue to the cardboard you are decorating.

Cardboard

Use mat board, cardboard backing from writing pads, shirt cardboard, and the like. Larger items require thicker cardboard. If thick cardboard is not readily available, or if your paper cutter will not make clean cuts through thick cardboard, you can make your own thick cardboard by cutting two or more pieces of thin cardboard to the same size and gluing them together.

Cutting Tools

Cardboard must be cut accurately. If a paper cutter is not available, use a mat knife with a sharp blade. Sharpen or replace the blade often. You must use a metal-edged ruler and a carpenter's metal right angle when cutting with a mat knife. These cutting guides are available with nonslip cork backing. Always work on extra layers of cardboard to protect the table while cutting. Put pressure on the ruler rather than the mat knife and cut through the cardboard in two or more strokes.

Paper and fabric may be cut with scissors only along edges that will not be exposed in the finished product. Otherwise, scissors are used primarily for trimming excess paper and cloth from corners that have to be mitered in order to reduce bulk.

Glue

White glue, such as Sobo or Elmer's, is best to use because it is quick-drying and can be used on paper, bookcloth, fabric, and cardboard.

Mix the white glue with water so that it can be brushed on easily. Keep the thinned glue in a shallow plastic container and cover tightly when not in use. (For certain applications you will need very thick glue: set out a little undiluted glue for an hour or two until some of the water in it has evaporated.) To clean glue containers, allow empty containers to dry out completely and peel off the glue.

If a slower-drying adhesive is desired, a wheat-paste mixture may be used instead. Sprinkle two tablespoons of wheat paste over one-half a cup of water. Let it stand for five minutes until thickened. Brush the paste on the paper, let it stand a few minutes, and apply another coat. The paper will then lie flat and will be easy to handle. Weight items that are pasted in this way until they dry to prevent warping. This paste, however, is not recommended for bookcloth or fabric. It should be discarded after a few days.

When gluing or pasting, place the paper or fabric face down on a piece of waste sheet, such as newspaper or pages from an old telephone directory. After each piece is glued, discard the waste sheet. Use waste sheets only once.

Use a flat varnish brush or an oil-painting bristle brush to apply the glue. The proper size of the brush depends on the area you wish to cover. To avoid getting glue on the right side of the decorative material, hold it firmly in place and brush the glue from the center of the piece towards the edges. It is often impossible to keep from getting a little glue on the fingers, so keep a damp cloth or sponge handy.

Air bubbles become trapped between two glued surfaces, and must be smoothed out. Bookbinding bone folders (1–1), available at library-supply outlets, are excellent for this purpose. A tongue depressor is also suitable, although it may be a little more tiring to work with. However, it is conveniently available and inexpensive if you are working with a large group. A bone folder or tongue depressor is also necessary for applying concentrated pressure to bulky areas, such as covered corners, in order to make them lie flat. It may be helpful at times to place a piece of white paper between the bone folder and the material being rubbed to prevent damage.

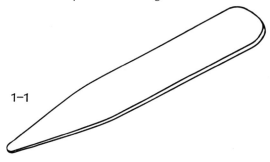

1–1

List of Tools and Materials Needed for All Items

Decorative papers and/or bookcloth or fabric
Cardboard
Wastepaper
Paper cutter or mat knife
Metal-edged ruler and metal right angle.
Scissors
White glue
Flat varnish or oil-painting bristle brushes
Bookbinder's bone folder or tongue depressor

Grain

Paper, like wood, has a *grain*. Paper folds most easily along its grain lines (1–2), so when you plan the layout for an item you are constructing you should take this grain into consideration. If you cut decorative papers with the grain running lengthwise (parallel to the longer dimension), most of the folds in the paper will be parallel to the paper's grain. For example, a paper hinge, described in Chapter 3, must fold along the paper's grain lines, or it will not have a neat appearance.

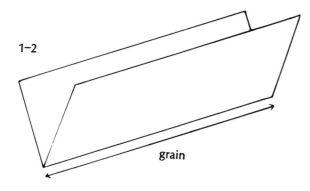

1–2

grain

Take a piece of paper—any piece will do—and tear it in half. Fold one piece parallel to the tear, and the other perpendicular to the tear. You should notice that one of the pieces is easier to fold, and that the fold line is cleaner. If you see no difference, try a heavier piece of paper.

You may also determine the grain of a piece of paper by dampening a small piece of it; it will curl up parallel to the grain lines (1–3).

Cardboard also has a grain. Since cardboard is stiffer than paper it is not practical actually to fold it in order to determine its grain. Instead, take a piece of cardboard and bend two of its opposite edges a little towards each other. Note the resistance. Now bend the remaining opposite edges together. The cardboard bends or curls most easily along the grain lines. Cardboard is usually cut with the grain running lengthwise for reasons pertaining to stress and leverage.

Commercial bookcloth also has a grain; like paper, it bends and folds most easily along its grain lines. Put a piece of bookcloth in a damp place, and it will curl as in figure 1–3. It is essential that any hinge made of bookcloth be constructed so that the fold is parallel to the grain. In planning the construction of an item, this takes priority over every other consideration of grain placement. Otherwise, if there is no hinge, the grain should run lengthwise.

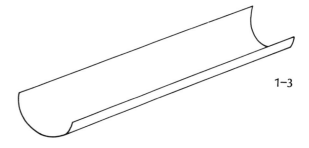

1–3

Try to cut cardboard, cloth, and paper so that the grain of pieces to be glued together will run in the same direction. At times this rule may be violated, especially if the design does not run with the grain and you are using lightweight paper or dressmakers' fabric. But—all *hinges* must be cut so that they fold along the grain.

2. Flat Decorative Items

Surprisingly attractive and useful items may be made by doing little more than covering a flat piece of cardboard with decorative paper or fabric. Try some of the ideas suggested in this chapter, or invent some of your own.

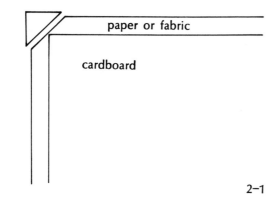

2–1

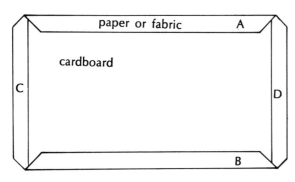

2–2

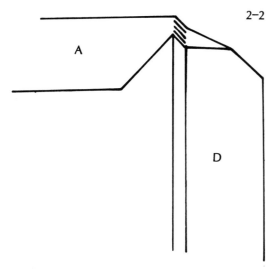

2–3

Cut a piece of decorative paper or paper-lined fabric larger than the piece of cardboard to be covered. The covering material is usually cut so that ½″ to ¾″ can be turned over each edge, less for very small items, and more for very large ones.

Lay the decorative material right side down on a piece of waste sheet. Apply glue to the wrong side of the entire material. Remove the piece of waste sheet. Center the piece of cardboard to be covered on the glued paper or fabric.

Miter all four corners: cut a triangle of the covering material about ⅛″ from the corner of the cardboard, shown as in figure 2–1. Mitering corners reduces bulk at the corners when the covering material is finally folded over. Be careful not to miter too close to the cardboard; a small margin of covering material is needed to ensure complete covering of the corner.

Fold over edges A and B (2–2), and smooth with a bookbinder's bone folder or tongue depressor.

Press the mitered edge of the paper or fabric (the shaded area in 2–3) around the edge of the cardboard with your fingernail. This step neatly hides the small excess of covering material that was left to ensure complete coverage of the corner, and is the key to a neat-looking corner.

Fold over edges C and D, and smooth with a bone folder.

Press down on the finished corners with the bone folder to smooth out their bulk.

Turn the covered piece over and smooth out any air bubbles. You may place a protective piece of white paper over the covered cardboard while you are smoothing out the air bubbles.

Basic Technique #2/Lining a Piece of Covered Board

If you apply decorative paper or fabric to one side of a piece of cardboard and leave the other side unfinished, you will notice that the cardboard curls along its grain as the glue dries. Therefore it is necessary to glue a lining to all covered pieces in order to produce a counter force, which will result in a flat item when the glue is dry (several hours).

Cut a piece of paper or cloth slightly smaller than the piece of covered cardboard you wish to line.

Apply glue to the wrong side of this lining material.

Apply the lining to the uncovered side of the cardboard, centering carefully (2–4).

Smooth with a bone folder.

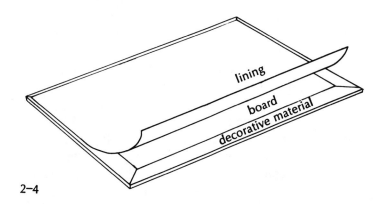

2–4

2-5

A looseleaf notebook covered with decorative paper. A design was carved out of a soap eraser with a mat knife. The eraser was then inked on an ink pad and stamped on paper in an allover design.

A Looseleaf Notebook (2–5)

This type of binder can hold photographs or serve as a scrapbook. It can be made in a variety of sizes; these directions are for a notebook 5¼″ x 6¼″.

Special materials: two looseleaf rings; ribbon, yarn, or cord; filler paper or other heavy paper

Special tool: awl or paper punch

Cut pieces of construction paper or other filler paper to size 5″ x 6″, with the grain running lengthwise.

Cut two pieces of cardboard ¼″ larger than the pages (5¼″ x 6¼″), with the grain running lengthwise.

Cut two pieces of decorative paper 1¼″ larger than the cardboard (6½″ x 7½″), with the grain running lengthwise.

Cover each piece of cardboard with the decorative paper (refer to Basic Technique #1).

Line each covered piece of cardboard with a 5″ x 6″ sheet of the filler paper used in the binder, centering carefully (Basic Technique #2).

Carefully mark the location of the ring holes with a pencil dot on the right side of each piece of the covered board.

Punch the ring holes from the right side of the covered boards with an awl or paper punch.

Mark the pages for holes and punch out. Assemble the binder with rings or ribbon.

An Accordion Booklet (2–6)

This seven-fold booklet is attached to a cover at each end.

Cut a strip of paper 24″ x 5″ with the grain parallel to the shorter dimension.

2-6

Oriental paper is used on the covers of this accordion booklet.

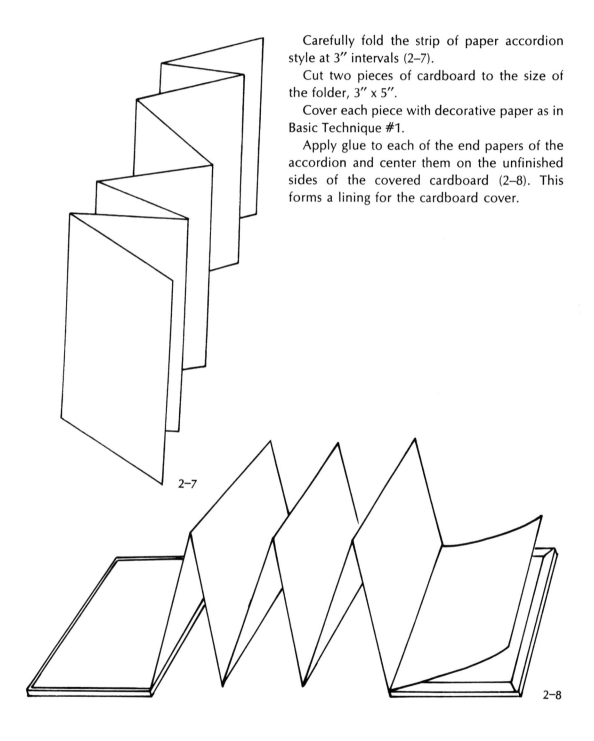

Carefully fold the strip of paper accordion style at 3″ intervals (2–7).

Cut two pieces of cardboard to the size of the folder, 3″ x 5″.

Cover each piece with decorative paper as in Basic Technique #1.

Apply glue to each of the end papers of the accordion and center them on the unfinished sides of the covered cardboard (2–8). This forms a lining for the cardboard cover.

2–7

2–8

An Accordion File (2–9)

A purchased file is bound in boards covered with decorative paper and closed with ribbon.

Special materials: purchased accordion file; two 15″ lengths of ribbon

Special tool: paper punch, wood chisel, or awl

Cut two pieces of cardboard about ¼″ larger than the face of the file.

Cut two pieces of decorative paper about 1½″ larger than the cardboard covers.

Cover each piece of cardboard with a piece of decorative paper as in Basic Technique #1.

Cut a slit the width of the ribbon near the top of each piece of covered board with a hammer and chisel (2–10).

Pull about ½″ of ribbon through each hole and glue it to the wrong side with thick glue (2–11).

Line each piece of covered cardboard to prevent warping. (Gluing the unlined boards directly to the file does not prevent warping, because of the type of cardboard used to make these files).

Glue the finished covers to the purchased file. Press firmly and hold together with spring-type clothespins until the glue sets.

2-9

Gift-wrap paper on a purchased accordion file.

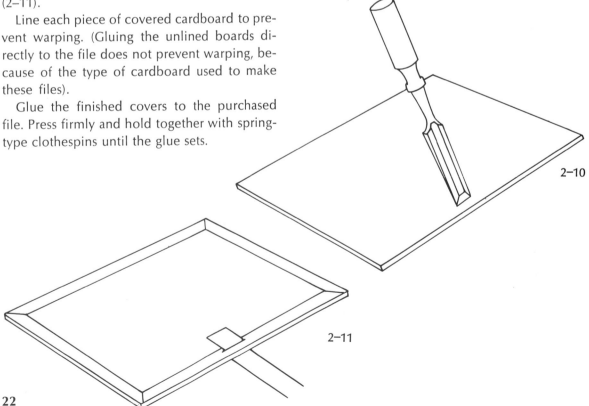

2–10

2–11

22

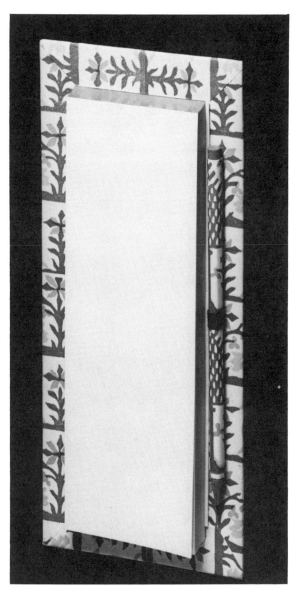

2-12

The repeated pattern on the paper on this wall pad with matching pencil could be made with a carved eraser, linoleum block, or potato.

A Wall Pad with Matching Pencil (2–12)

The pad holder is cut larger than the pad to accommodate the pencil and to show off the matching decorative paper.

Special materials: long shopping pad; pencil; 2" length of narrow ribbon; needle and thread to match ribbon; mounting squares with adhesive on both sides

Cut a piece of decorative paper a little wider than the circumference of the pencil. The grain should run lengthwise so that the paper will tend to curl around the pencil (2–13).

Apply glue to the pencil covering and position the pencil immediately on the paper to prevent the paper from curling excessively (2–14). Wait a short while before actually rolling the pencil up in the paper; once the glue becomes tacky it will adhere more readily to the shiny coating on the pencil.

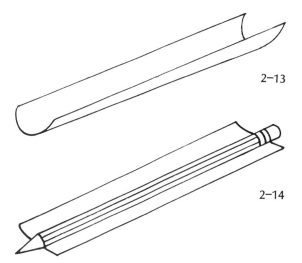

2-13

2-14

Smooth the seam with a bone folder.

Wrap the piece of ribbon around the pencil and stitch the loop with a needle and thread (2–15). The pencil should slide easily through the loop without actually dropping out.

Cut the cardboard to the size you have determined and cover with decorative paper as in Basic Technique #1. Line with paper or bookcloth as in Basic Technique #2.

Glue the ribbon to the back of the pad with heavy glue (2–16). The stitching line on the ribbon should protrude just a little from the edge of the pad. Glue the pad in place on the covered board.

Apply the double-faced adhesive backing to the back of the covered board (2–17).

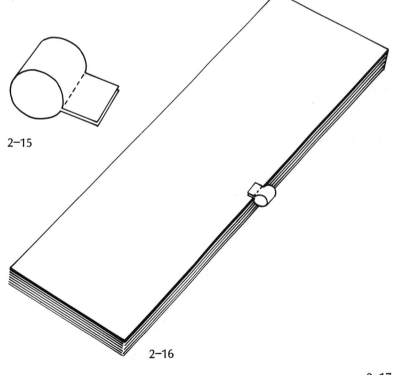

2–15

2–16

2–17

24

2-18

A crayon drawing decorates the paper for this paper clip.

A Paper Clip (2–18)

Special materials: spring-type clothespin

Cut two pieces of cardboard to the shape desired; a trapezoid is shown here.

Cut the decorative paper and lining material to the sizes required to cover and line the cardboard shapes.

Glue the decorative paper to the cardboard as in Basic Technique #1, mitering the corners (2–19).

Glue the lining to the other side as in Basic Technique #2.

Glue the clothespin to the boards with thick glue.

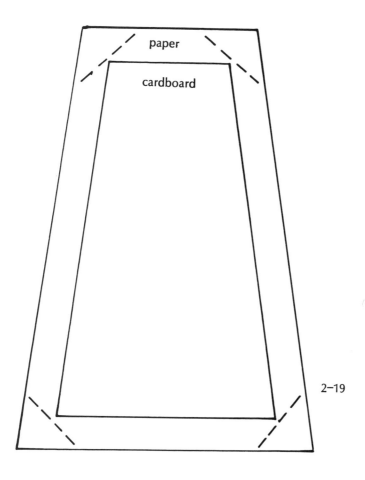

paper

cardboard

2–19

A Wall Clipboard (2–20)

Each of the two clothespins is attached with one side glued to one covered shape and then the other side glued to the wallboard. The back of the board is lined, and has mounting squares on it so that it can be attached to a wall.

2-20

A thumb print defined with pen and ink and feathered with paintbrush strokes becomes a bird for the paper decorating a wall clipboard.

A Desk-Blotter Holder with Four Corners (2–21)

This blotter holder has four corners that are covered with decorative paper to match other desk accessories.

Cut a piece of cardboard backing the desired size of the blotter holder and a piece of book-cloth two inches larger than the cardboard.

Trim the corners (2–22) so that unnecessary bulk at the corners will be eliminated.

Glue the cloth to the cardboard backing.

Turn down the edges and glue (2–23).

Determine the size of the triangular corners and cut a pattern out of thin cardboard.

Cut four triangular pieces of bookcloth ⅝″ larger than each side of the triangle.

2-21

Geometric designs on decorative paper accent the corners of this desk-blotter holder covered with bookcloth.

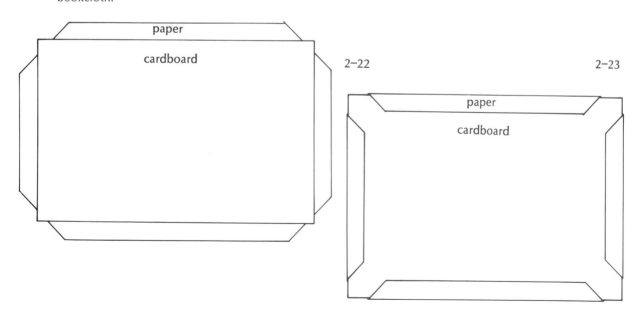

paper

cardboard

2-22

2-23

paper

cardboard

Trace the triangular pattern on each one (2–24).

Fold along the base of the triangle (2–25) and glue down the hem. Trim as in figure 2–26.

Cut a piece of bookcloth or paper slightly smaller than the pattern and glue to the inside to prevent warping (2–27).

Miter the apex (2–27), glue, and fold the remaining edges over the covered backing board (2–28 and 2–29), making sure that the corner of the board is placed on the pencil area representing the triangular pattern. Repeat for the other three corners.

Cut a lining for the back of the blotter holder and apply as in Basic Technique #2.

Cut four triangles of decorative paper to apply to the cloth corners. Cut these paper triangles so that a ⅛" border of bookcloth is visible when the blotter is in place.

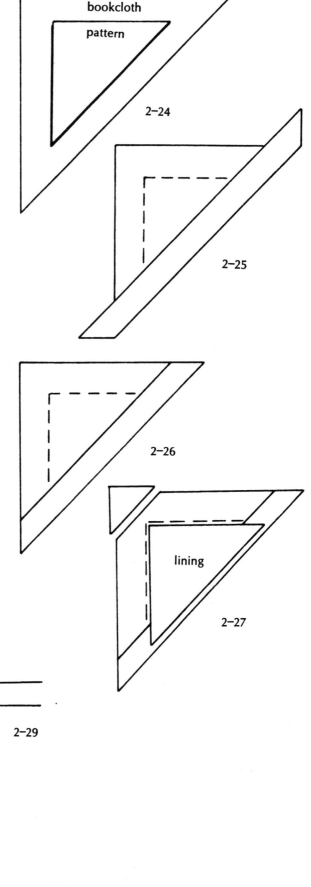

bookcloth

pattern

2–24

2–25

2–26

lining

2–27

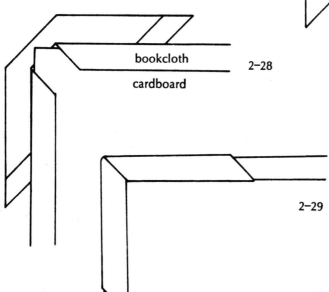

bookcloth   2–28

cardboard

2–29

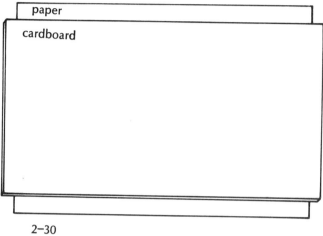

2–30

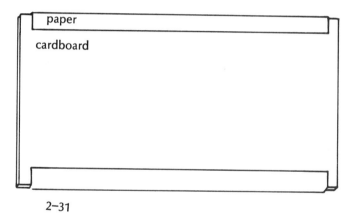

2–31

A Desk-Blotter Holder with Vertical Panels (C–1)

Cut heavy cardboard for the backing piece, or cut two pieces of mat board the same size and glue them together.

Cut decorative paper to cover most of the backing piece (2–30).

Glue the paper in place, turn over the edges and glue them to the back (2–31).

Determine the width of the two vertical panels and cut two strips out of thin cardboard to this width and as long as the height of the backing board.

Cut bookcloth ⅝″ larger on each side to cover these strips.

Apply glue to the wrong side of one of the bookcloth strips, center a piece of cardboard on it, and turn over one edge (2–32).

Add a facing or lining of bookcloth to prevent warping (2–33).

Miter two corners, as shown in figure 2–34, a little more than ⅛″ from the cardboard.

Glue the panel to the backing as shown in 2–35 and 2–36.

Repeat for the other retaining panel and line the back.

2–32

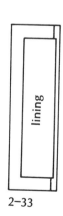

2–33

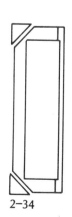

2–34

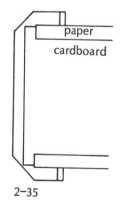

2–35

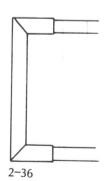

2–36

3. The Single Hinge

You can make a great variety of interesting items with hinged parts. The single hinge, introduced in this chapter, is made between two pieces of cardboard that have been cut to the same length. The hinge material itself may be of paper or fabric, and must be applied with its grain parallel to the fold line of the hinge. Basic Technique #3 produces a flat booklet with two covers. Basic Technique #4 is used to make one or more single hinged covers to enclose a thicker item.

Cut a piece of bookcloth for the hinge with the grain running lengthwise. Cut this piece 1″ wide and about 5″ long. Apply glue to the hinge and place two pieces of cardboard about 2″ x 3¾″ on it about ⅛″ apart (3–1). If the cardboard is very heavy, or if the hinge must bend through 180°, you will need to leave a gap larger than ⅛″. Turn over the edges of the hinge, and press along the groove with the bone folder (3–2).

Cut a lining for the hinge with the grain running lengthwise. It should be about as wide as the piece of bookcloth and a little shorter than the finished hinge.

Glue the lining in place and press the lining into the groove.

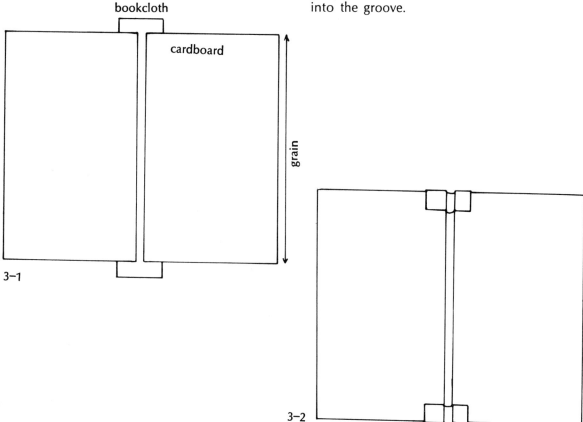

bookcloth

cardboard

grain

3–1

3–2

Cut a piece of cloth or paper for the hinge and board as shown in either 3–3 or 3–4. In 3–4 only the hinge and a piece of the cardboard are covered; in 3–3, the hinge and the whole cardboard are covered with the same decorative material. Here, as elsewhere, you can cover any remaining cardboard with any decorative material of your choice, using Basic Technique #1 and 2. The grain must run as shown.

Apply glue to the hinge material and place the pieces of cardboard about ⅛″ apart on it. The amount of space allowed depends on the weight of the material used and the thickness of the board.

Miter the corners and fold over all edges.

Press the covered grooves with the bone folder.

Cut a lining for the hinge and apply to the inside, pressing between the grooves.

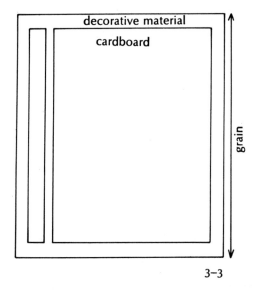

3–3

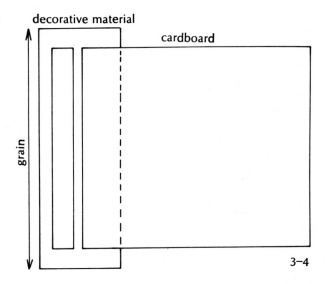

3–4

3-5

Whimsical batik design on a hinged photograph album. (Fabric by Anne Feidelson)

A Hinged Photograph Album (3–5)

Special materials: construction paper or other heavy paper for the pages; ribbon or yarn

Cut cardboard for the cover: two pieces 7″ x 9″ and two hinge pieces 1″ x 7″. See figure 3–3 for grain placement.

Cut two pieces of cloth as indicated in figure 3–3.

Apply glue to the board and lay the board on the fabric.

Miter the corners, glue the edges, and turn them down.

Cut the filler paper slightly smaller than the finished cardboard covers.

Punch holes in the filler paper and the covers.

Line each cover with one sheet of filler paper, pressing the lining into the groove.

Tie the covers together with ribbon or yarn.

A Large Photo Album (C–2)

The covers (prepared as in 3–3) are measured and cut slightly larger than purchased refill paper for a large photograph album. A solid color covers the entire back cover. Bookcloth is used to line the inside covers.

A Photo Album with Inverted Hinges (3–6)

In this design the hinges are turned inside before being attached to the filler paper. The space for the hinge between the pieces of cardboard should be about ¼" or more to allow the hinge to bend completely under. Holes were punched and posts used to connect the covers to the pages. In this example bookcloth and paper are used as in figure 3–4.

3-6

A photo album with inverted hinges, covered with bookcloth and decorative paper.

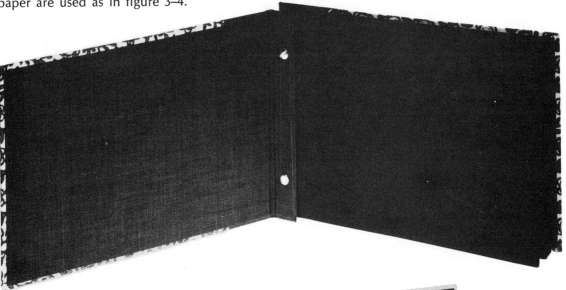

A Large Photo Album Covered with Fabric (3–7)

This cover with inverted hinges is made as shown in figure 3–3.

3-7

The fabric covering on this large photo album was printed by silk screen. (Designed and executed by Gigi Wolff, age 10)

34

3-8

A book stand covered with decorative paper.

A Book Stand (3–8)

Two bookcloth hinges (made as in Basic Technique #3) connect three heavy cardboard panels, which are then covered with decorative paper and lined. A length of purchased molding is covered with decorative paper and is then glued to the middle panel (3–9). A thick strip of cardboard is covered with decorative paper and glued to the first panel (3–10). The stand is assembled as shown in figure 3–11.

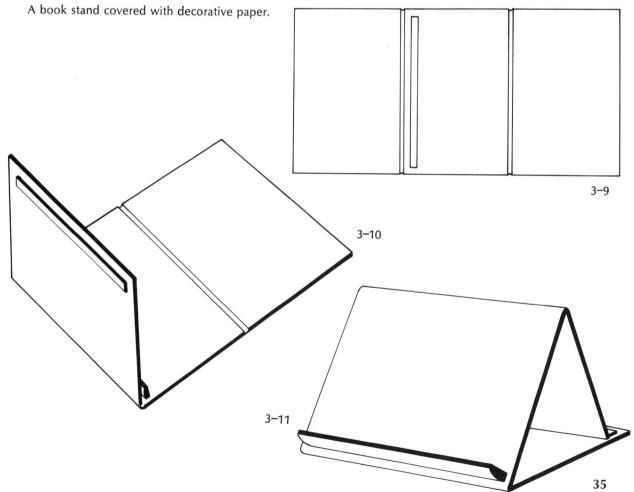

3–9

3–10

3–11

A Scrap Basket (3–12)

This scrap basket is made out of four pieces of double-thickness mat board, each 7″ x 10½″.

Attach the four panels to three strips of book-cloth ⅜″ x 12″ as in Basic Technique #3 (3–13). Leave at least ¼″ between the panels, or enough space so that one panel can be turned over on the other. Turn down the edges and glue to the other side.

Turn the four panels over and glue decorative paper to the outside of each panel between the bookcloth hinges, overlapping the book-cloth slightly (3–14).

Turn down the edges at the top and bottom and glue to the other side. Turn the four panels over.

Measure and cut three linings out of book-cloth slightly shorter than the height of the basket. They should be wide enough to cover one panel plus the hinge plus ½″ of the next panel (3–15).

Overlap the second panel lining on the end of the first. Cut the fourth lining the width of the fourth panel only.

3-12

A scrap basket covered with Italian decorative paper.

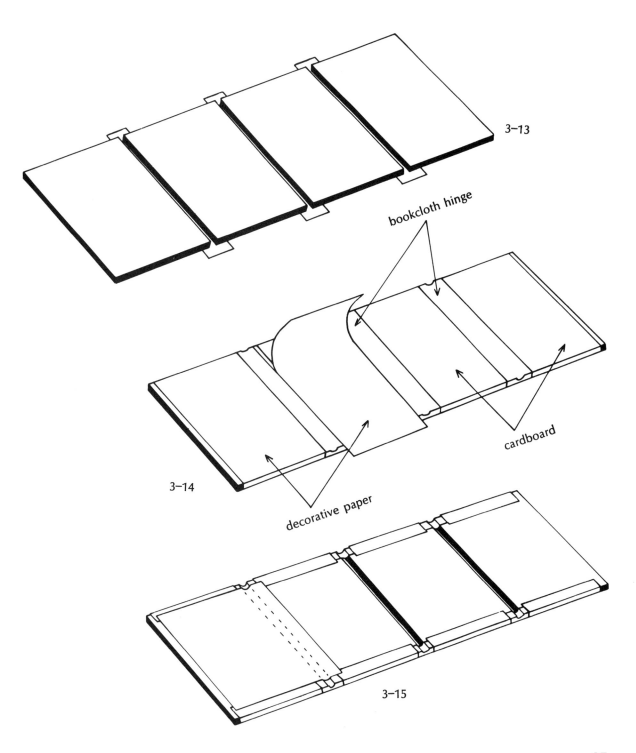

3–13

bookcloth hinge

cardboard

3–14

decorative paper

3–15

37

Fold the panels over right side out in order to connect the first and fourth panels. Glue a fourth strip of bookcloth ¾" wide by 12" long on the wrong side and place under the first and fourth panels (3–16).

Turn the ends down. Reach inside carefully and check to see that the bookcloth strip has adhered to the inside.

Cut an outside strip ¾" wide and the length of the board (10½") and glue to the other side.

Prepare four strips of double thickness mat board ½" wide by 6½" long. Cut four pieces of paper or bookcloth 6½" long and wide enough to go around the strip. Glue to the strips as in figures 3–17 and 3–18.

Turn the basket upside down and glue one of the strips to the inside of each side with thick glue (3–19), holding it in place with a clothespin. This becomes the ledge on which to rest the bottom of the basket.

When the strips have adhered, turn the basket right side up and measure, cover, and line a board that will rest on the ledge and fit snugly. It is not necessary to glue the bottom to the ledge. If it is done, however, the glue should be put on the ledge.

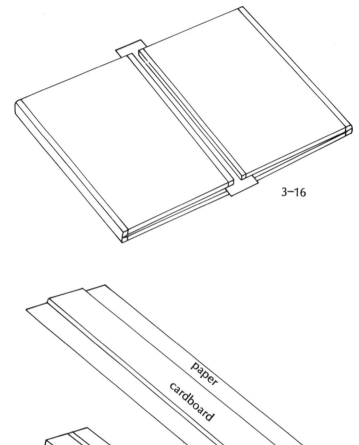

3–16

paper

cardboard

3–17

3–18

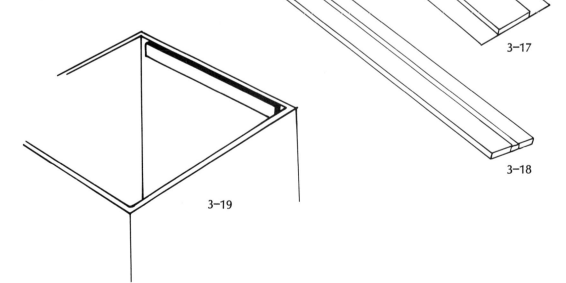

3–19

3-20

A Folding Desk Basket (3–20)

Cover four pieces of cardboard with one piece of bookcloth, leaving a hinge space between the cardboard panels (3–21). Turn the edges down and glue. This is the inside.

Cut decorative paper about ⅜" shorter than the height of the boards and glue to the uncovered side of the four panels (3–22). This is the outside of the box.

Hinge the first and fourth panels together as in 3–16, connecting them with bookcloth on the inside and matching patterns when cutting the decorative paper for the outside strip. The bottom of the basket is made as in figure 3–12.

In the example shown in figure 3–20, the cardboard was cut to a size that would allow the design on the decorative paper to be centered on each panel.

A design like the one on this folding desk box could be made with a linoleum block.

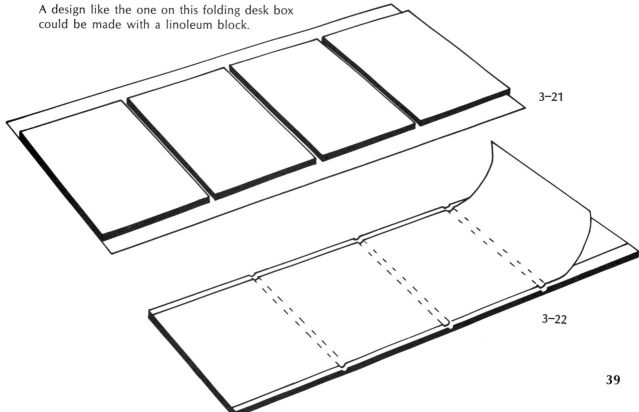

3–21

3–22

4. The Hard-Spine Double Hinge

A double hinge has a cardboard spine between the two pieces of cardboard being hinged together; there is a single hinge, as discussed in the previous chapter, between the spine and each piece of cardboard. These double hinges are ordinarily used to cover pads or boxes. The size of the pieces of cardboard is determined by the size of the item to be covered, and the width of the spine is determined by the exact thickness of the item.

Cut a strip of cardboard the length of the two pieces of cardboard to be hinged together. It should be exactly as wide as the depth of the finished item which is being covered (such as the thickness of a pad). The grain on this spine must run lengthwise (4–1).

Cut the hinge material, allowing for the width of the spine, two gaps of about ⅛″ between the boards, the width of the border desired on the front and back, and for any overlap you may require (4–2). (The hinge material can be cut to cover all three pieces of cardboard, or decorative paper can be used to cover the front and back.)

Cut a hinge lining as wide as the outer hinge material, and a little shorter than the finished length of the board.

Apply glue to the hinge material, and place the boards and the spine on it, leaving a space of about ⅛″ between each piece.

Turn over the edges of the hinge material and line with the hinge lining.

4–1

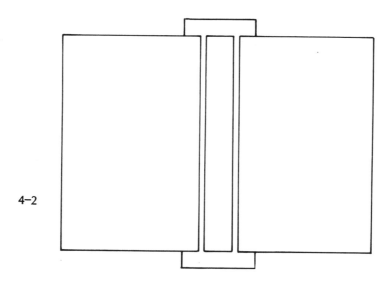

4–2

A Note-pad Cover (4–3)

Cut two cardboard covers 3⅛″ x 5¼″ and a spine ¼″ x 5¼″. The grain should run lengthwise.

Cut a hinge of bookcloth with the grain running lengthwise (1¾″ x 6½″) and a lining for the spine out of bookcloth (1¾″ x 5″).

Assemble the hinge as in Basic Technique #5.

Cut the decorative paper so that it will overlap the bookcloth slightly. Allow ⅝″ on the remaining three sides as shown in figure 4–4.

For accuracy in gluing the decorative paper, close the cover (4–5) and apply the glued paper to the boards. Be careful to glue it parallel to the edge of the spine.

Turn down the edges and glue as in Basic Technique #1.

Glue the pad in place on the inside right-hand cover close to the spine.

Cut a piece of white paper slightly narrower than the width of the pad and glue it to the inside of the left cover.

If you wish to make a refillable note-pad cover, refer to Basic Technique #6 for directions on making a sleeve for a removable pad.

4-3

The gift-wrap paper on this note-pad cover suggests ideas for decorating with pen and ink.

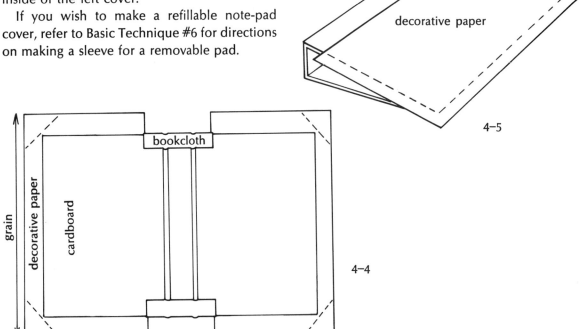

decorative paper

4–5

bookcloth

grain

decorative paper

cardboard

4–4

4-6

A Double Pad Cover (4–6)

The cover illustrated is made of fabric and holds two standard 3″ x 5″ pads.

Cut the two pieces of cardboard and the spine. The spine should be the width of the combined thickness of the two pads.

Apply glue to the boards and place them on the fabric (4–7).

Miter the corners, glue and turn down the edges, and line the spine.

Glue a pad to the inside of each cover.

A holder for two pads covered with an India print fabric.

4–7

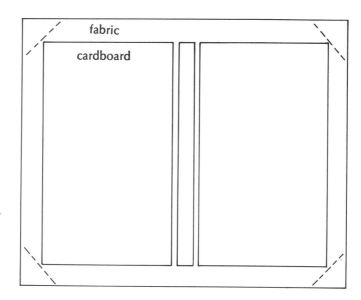

Basic Technique #6/Making a Sleeve for a Removable Pad

4–8

Cut the sleeve from a good-quality paper so that the fold will be parallel to the grain. The sleeve should be about ¼" shorter than the pad, and about ½" wider than double the width of the pad.

Fold the sleeve around the back of the pad and tape it in place (4–8). Be sure that the pad will slide easily into it.

Glue the sleeve onto the inside of the pad cover, while the pad is in the sleeve, taking care not to get glue too near the open edges of the sleeve. This sleeve also forms a lining for the board to which it is glued.

A Note-pad Cover with Postcard (4–9)

The covering for the two boards and hinge are cut in one piece out of bookcloth as in figure 4–7, and a picture postcard is glued to the front cover.

4-9

A postcard reproduction of a Picasso is used on this desk pad holder.

4-10

A playing card decorates this pad cover.

A Note-pad Cover with Playing Card (4–10)

A Note-pad Cover with Collage (4–11)

A tissue-paper collage on bookcloth covers a 5″ x 8″ note pad. Ten or more layers of colored tissue paper are cut at one time into rhythmical shapes. When separated they are arranged on bookcloth that is first coated with acrylic polymer emulsion.

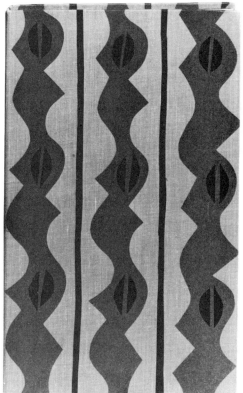

4-11

A note-pad cover with a tissue-paper collage.

4-12

Marbled paper is used to cover this tiny matchbox.

A Tiny Matchbox (4–12)

Cover a matchbox as you would cover a pad. This purchased novelty matchbox, when glued to both covers, serves as a lining (4–13).

A Writing Tablet with Inside Pocket (4–14)

Cut the cloth for the hinge and back cover in one piece (4–15).

Add the decorative paper on the front cover, mitering the corners.

Attach a pocket made of decorative paper as in figures 2–32 through 2–36. Note that the lining for the front cover and the hinge is cut in one piece (4–16). The sleeve for the note pad forms the lining for the back cover.

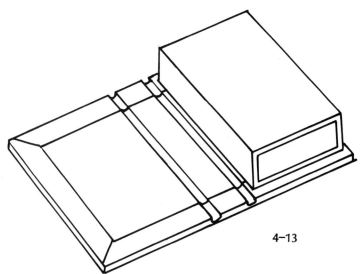

4–13

4-14

A writing tablet covered with marbled paper, with a matching inside pocket.

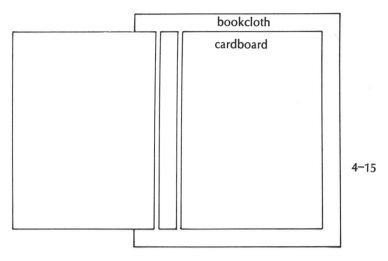

bookcloth

cardboard

4–15

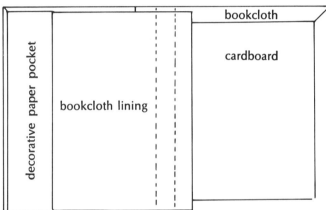

decorative paper pocket

bookcloth

cardboard

bookcloth lining

4–16

4-17

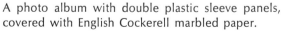

A photo album with double plastic sleeve panels, covered with English Cockerell marbled paper.

A Photo Album with Double Plastic Sleeve Panels (4–17)

A Photo Album with Plastic Sleeves (C–3)
This batik-covered album has a panel of rectangular photo sleeves glued to the inside of each cover. The panels are available at most stationery stores.

5. The Soft-Spine Double Hinge

A soft-spine double hinge is made essentially like a hard-spine double-hinge, as in Basic Technique #5, except that the cardboard is left out of the spine. In its place an additional strip of bookcloth or heavy paper may be used to give the hinge more body, so that, for example, this hinge may be used when making a reusable cover for paperback books, which may not all be of the same bulk, or thickness.

Determine the width of the hinge. It must be wider than the finished thickness of the item to be covered, because the hinge is soft and will curve outward. The exact width of the hinge depends upon both the weight of the bookcloth or fabric used and the thickness desired for the finished article. Usually the hinge will be about one third again as wide as the finished thickness desired, and even a little wider than that for narrow flexible hinges, or when heavy bookcloth is used to make the hinge. It is best to make a sample and test the width before proceeding.

Cut the hinge piece with the grain running lengthwise.

Glue the boards and hinge in place (5–1). When thin fabric is used for the hinge, cut an extra piece of bookcloth to fit between the cardboard. (Several sheets of paper glued together will also serve this purpose, but they must also be cut with the grain running lengthwise.)

Cut a lining for the hinge and glue it in place, pressing well with a bone folder into the groove (5–2).

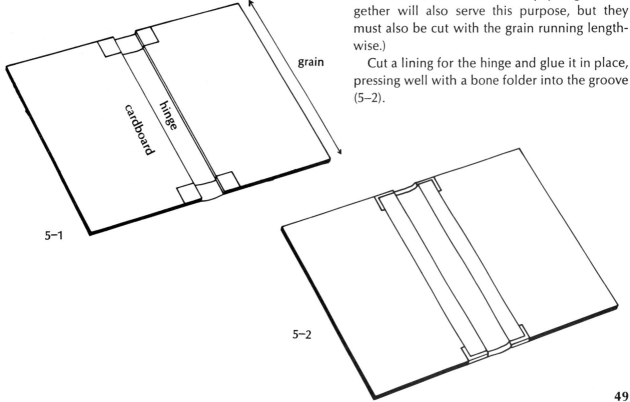

grain

hinge

cardboard

5–1

5–2

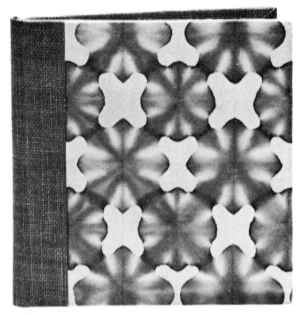

5-3

Photo holder for four pictures, covered with Oriental paper.

A Photo Folder for Four Pictures (5–3)

Special materials: two plastic 3½"-square photo holders from a card of photo sleeves, with the tapes attached.

Cut two pieces of cardboard 3¾" x 3¾" for the covers. Cut a piece of bookcloth 5" x 5⅜" to cover the spine and back, with the grain running with the shorter dimension.

Cut a soft spine of bookcloth ½" wide by 3¾" high.

Glue the two boards and the soft spine to the wrong side of the bookcloth as in figure 4–15.

Miter the corners, fold over, and glue.

Cut a piece of bookcloth for the hinge lining and apply it as in figure 5–2.

Cut a piece of decorative paper 4⅜" x 5" and glue it to the front cover, overlapping the book-cloth margin by ⅟₁₆" as in figure 4–5.

Tape a plastic photo holder to the inside of each of the covers so that the tape works as a hinge (5–4).

Cut two pieces of white lining paper a little smaller than the photo holders and glue them in place under the photo holders (5–4).

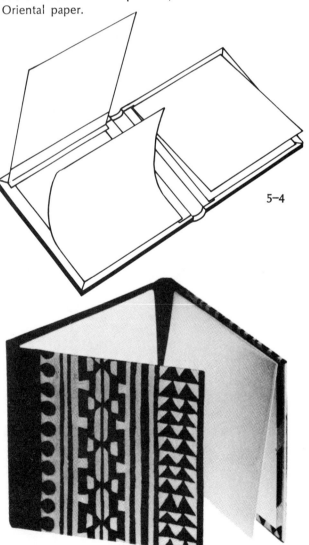

5-4

A Triple Photo Folder (5–5)

This is made like the double photo folder except that there are three panels used, necessitating two hinges. Each of the two side panels is covered with decorative paper.

5-5

A triple photo holder covered with oriental decorative paper.

5-6

Linen fabric is used on the outside of this checkbook cover. Bookcloth in a solid color is the lining.

A Checkbook Cover (5–6)

Cut two pieces of cardboard about ⅜″ wider and longer than the checkbook.

Cover with cloth (4–7), leaving a ⅝″ space for the flexible hinge.

Cut the lining for the hinge and the covers in one piece about ¼″ smaller than the size of the decorated cover (5–7). Be sure AB is at least ¹⁄₁₆″ longer than the height of the checkbook being covered, so that the checkbook fits.

Cut two retaining straps of bookcloth 2¾″ wide and 1½″ longer than the lining (5–7).

Fold the straps over the lining and glue in place on the wrong side (5–8).

Glue the lining to the cover (5–9) and press firmly with the bone folder until the lining adheres. Press into the grooves. Insert the checkbook into the straps.

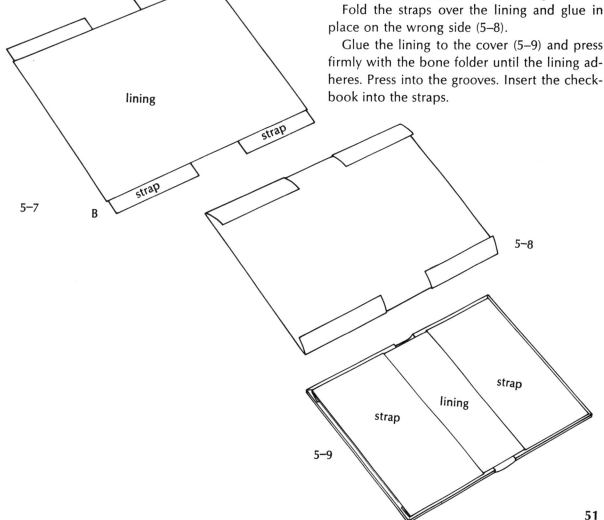

51

A Reusable Paperback Book Cover (5–10)
This cover is made like the checkbook cover. The straps can be narrower or wider, and should be placed ½″ from the spine on each side. This could also be used to cover a TV Guide or a magazine.

A Fabric Paperback Book Cover (C–4)

A Telephone-Directory Cover (C–5)
Although considerably larger than a checkbook, this telephone-directory cover is made in the same way as the checkbook cover, except that the straps are 4″ wide to accommodate the larger book.

5-10

Fold-and-dye paper on this paperback book cover.

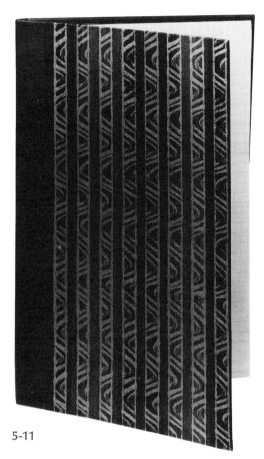

5-11

Paper batik design on a legal-pad holder.

A Legal-pad Holder (5–11)

Special material: 8″ x 12½″ legal pad

Cut two pieces of heavy cardboard 8½″ x 13″, or glue several pieces of cardboard together to make the covers thick.

Cut a soft spine of bookcloth or paper ⅝″ x 13″ to be used between the boards.

Cut decorative paper for the front cover.

Prepare the spine lining (12½″ high by 2″ wide).

Assemble the cover and hinge as in Basic Technique #5, using the method illustrated in figure 4–15.

Line the spine.

Cover the front with decorative paper as in figure 4–5.

Cut linings for the inside of bookcloth the size of the legal pad.

Cut a pattern out of thin cardboard the size and shape of the pocket. Prepare the bookcloth pocket (2–32 through 2–36), substituting the shapes shown in figure 5–12.

Glue the lining-pocket to the inside cover (5–12).

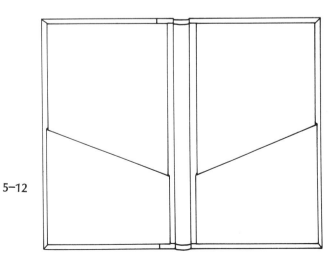

5–12

A Letter Portfolio (C–6)

This cover is made like the legal pad except that the decorative paper is used on both covers and for the pockets. The pockets are rectangles applied by the same principle as the legal-pad pockets.

A Three-Panel Writing Portfolio (C–7)

This versatile folder holds stationery and also serves as a lap desk. The outside cover is made like the photo folder in figure 5–5. The inside of the portfolio is shown in 5–13. The inside covers are made as in figure 4–16 (see 2–32 through 2–36). The triangles are attached to the bookcloth lining and are glued to the inside center panel (2–24 through 2–29).

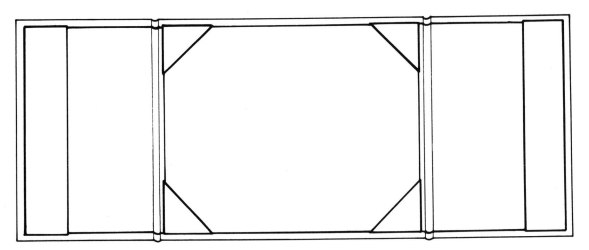

5–13

A Portfolio To Hold Drawings (C–8)

Follow the instructions given in Basic Technique #7 for making this type of cover. Before applying the lining (5–14) attach the ribbons as in figures 2–10 and 2–11.

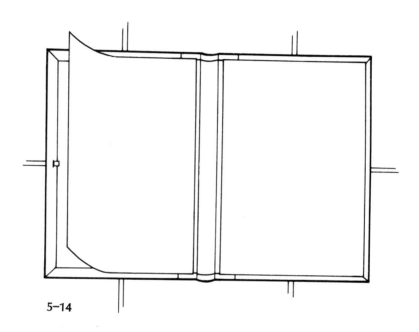

5–14

An Enclosed Portfolio (5–15)

Prepare the boards to the dimensions required as follows (5–16): A = C, B = D, E is half the width of A, and B is half the length of A. The space between the boards is about 1″.

Lay the parts on a large piece of bookcloth (5–17), allowing about 1″ for a soft spine on all four sides of A.

Trim the bookcloth, leaving ¾″ to turn in.

Glue the boards and the soft spines to the bookcloth. Turn over and bone down well.

Slit the corners (5–17), glue and turn down all edges. A triangular patch will be required at each of the four corners of A to cover the corners. This can be made of bookcloth.

Add the decorative paper (4–5).

Attach a lining of bookcloth to each flap (4–16) that will also cover the hinges. Last, glue the lining to A.

5-15

An enclosed portfolio accented with Italian decorative paper.

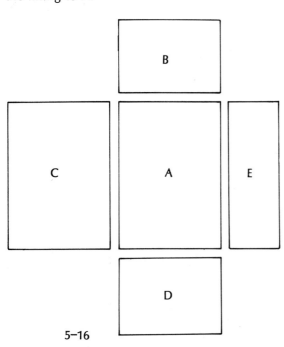

5–16

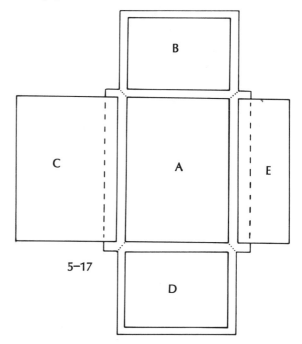

5–17

A Letter Portfolio (C–9)

This is a folder made of double thickness of cardboard connected by a soft hinge.

Cut four boards to the size required.

Glue two of them with bookcloth as in Basic Technique #1.

Glue decorative paper to one of the others.

To the fourth board glue decorative paper before adding a pocket lined with lightweight cardboard and covered with the same paper.

Connect the outside covers with a hinge of double-thickness bookcloth the length of the boards (5–18). Insert a piece of ribbon on each end before gluing each cover and lining together. Hold with spring-type clothespins until the glue is set.

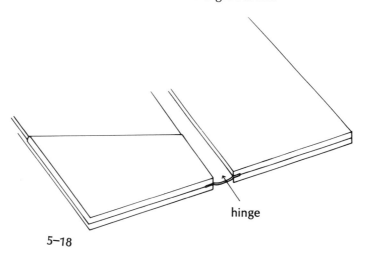

hinge

5–18

6. Binding a Book

Using the adaptation of traditional bookbinding described in Basic Technique #8, you can bind a favorite paperback in a hard cover, or make an attractive new binding for a hardbound book stripped of its old cover. No special equipment is needed, though great care must be taken to achieve professional results. Basic Technique #8 is designed for a book no more than ½" thick. For thicker books, the same procedure can be followed, but a soft-spine should be used instead of the hard spine.

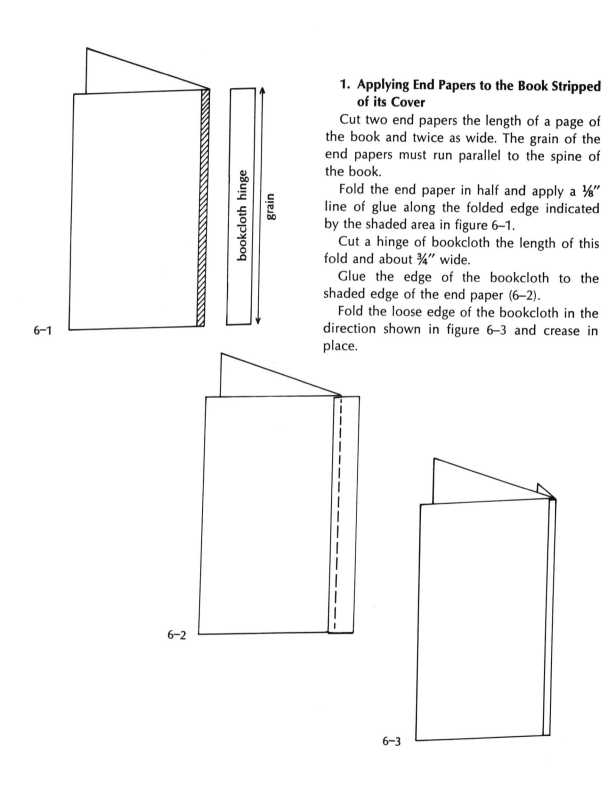

6-1

6-2

6-3

bookcloth hinge

grain

1. Applying End Papers to the Book Stripped of its Cover

Cut two end papers the length of a page of the book and twice as wide. The grain of the end papers must run parallel to the spine of the book.

Fold the end paper in half and apply a ⅛″ line of glue along the folded edge indicated by the shaded area in figure 6–1.

Cut a hinge of bookcloth the length of this fold and about ¾″ wide.

Glue the edge of the bookcloth to the shaded edge of the end paper (6–2).

Fold the loose edge of the bookcloth in the direction shown in figure 6–3 and crease in place.

Apply a line of glue ⅛″ wide along the glued edge of the cloth hinge and glue to the edge of the book (6–4 and 6–5).

Repeat for the other end paper.

Prepare a piece of lightweight bookcloth or fabric ¼″ shorter than the book and 1½″ wider than the spine. Apply glue to one side and attach it to the spine and the loose flaps of the end papers (6–6).

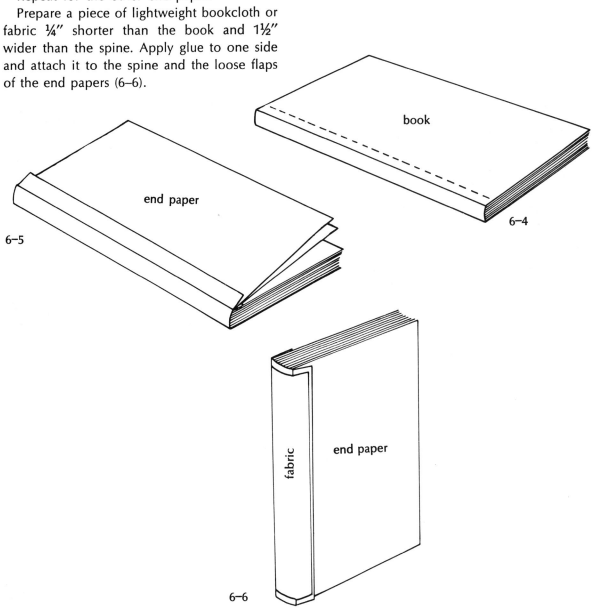

book

6–4

end paper

6–5

fabric

end paper

6–6

2. Attaching a Hard Cover to a Book that has been Prepared with End Papers

Cut the cardboard, bookcloth hinge, and decorative covering for the book. The spine must be the exact thickness of the book plus the cardboard covers yet to be put on (6–7). Remember that a soft spine should be used for a book more than ½″ thick. The boards may be wider than the book at this time, but will have to be trimmed later.

You must leave ¼″ spaces between the boards and the spine (6–8).

After gluing the two boards and the spine to the bookcloth, turn down the edges of the bookcloth and glue them to the inside of the cover.

Place the book with the end papers inside the covers and close the book to test the fit. Push the book firmly against the spine and run the bone folder along the indentation made by the ¼″ spaces (6–9).

At this time remove the book and trim the width of the cover so that the margins around the book are equal.

Add the decorative paper to each cover (4–5), glue down the edges, and bone well.

Apply thick glue to the ¼″ spaces between the boards to within ⅛″ of the top and bottom of the cover.

Place the book inside the cover firmly against the spine and close the book.

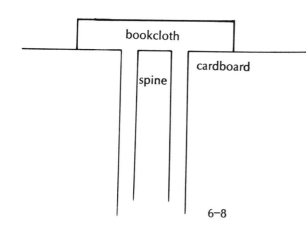

book

cardboard

6–7

bookcloth

spine   cardboard

6–8

Press along the indentation again on each side of the book (6–9) until the glue is set. This may take five minutes or more. This continuous pressure is normally applied by the brass-edged boards of a bookbinder's press, which can be used if available.

Open the cover and place a sheet of waste paper between the end papers A and B (6–10).

Apply glue to A and the loose part of the cloth hinge along C.

Remove the sheet of waste paper and close the book pressing firmly. A and C will adhere to the inside of the front cover, forming a lining.

Open the book only enough to permit your flattened hand to enter and smooth out any air bubbles that may still remain.

Place wax paper between the cover and the end paper B and leave it there until the glue is thoroughly dry. If the boards become warped at this time, place a heavy object or book on the cover. When the glue is dry, the cover will be flat.

Repeat for the end papers at the back of the book.

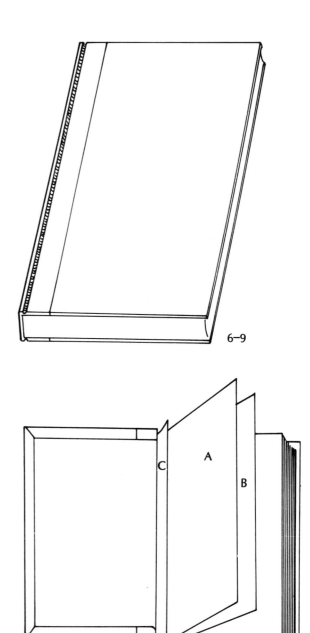

6–9

6–10

6-11

This 3" x 4" purchased address book is re-covered with a miniature wallpaper print.

An Address Book (6–11)

Small items like this are easy to work with and provide inexpensive material for experimenting with binding books.

The original cover of the address book is removed by cutting it with a mat knife on the dotted line (6–12) and is replaced with a new one (Basic Technique #8).

An Address Book with Decorative End Papers (6–13)

This book is prepared as explained in Basic Technique #8 except that the cover is made of bookcloth and the end papers are made of decorative paper.

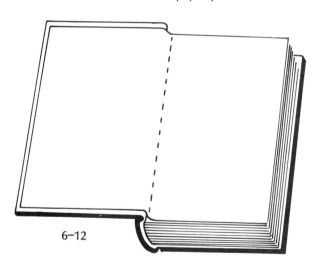

6-12

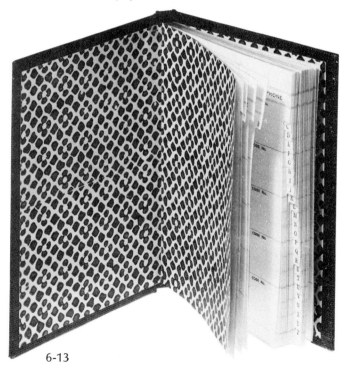

6-13

A hand-printed paper is used for the end papers of this address book, which is bound in a contrasting solid color.

A Re-Covered Paperback Book (6–14)

A new cover is made for a book of Matisse's work, using contrasting colors of bookcloth and paper. The tall rectangular portion on the left is bookcloth; the dark portion of the design is paper, on which two forms cut out of bookcloth were superimposed to form the background for the figure.

6-14

Cut paper on bookcloth is used on this re-covered paperback book. (Copy of a Matisse plate)

A Cloth-Covered Book (C–10)
A purchased blank-paged book is covered with a jersey print that is cut in one piece.

6-15

A linoleum block was used to make the repeat pattern on this book cover.

A Single-Signature Book (6–16)

Special materials: heavy thread; needle; awl; vellum stationery

Fold together seven or eight sheets of paper. These will become a signature. Be sure to fold along the grain (6–17). When these sheets are folded together, the inner pages will protrude slightly; these are trimmed later.

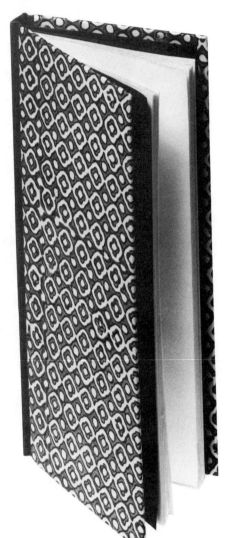

6-16

Italian decorative paper on a single-signature book.

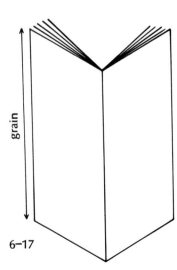

6–17

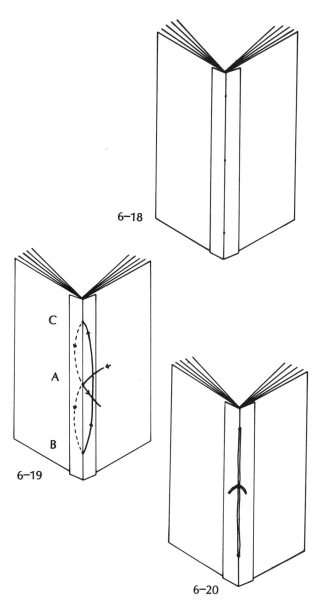

6–18

6–19

6–20

Cut a strip of bookcloth the length of the signature and fold it along the outside of the signature (6–18). Mark three dots on the outside of the fold.

Starting from the outside of the cloth strip, sew the paper and bookcloth together as follows (6–19): Sew through A to B. Bring the needle and thread around to the outside of the cloth and sew through C. Then sew through A again and tie the two ends of the thread together, enclosing thread BC (6–20).

Trim the booklet pages with a mat knife or paper cutter so that they are even, if you wish. Proceed to cover the book as in step 2 Basic Technique #8.

If colored end papers are to be used, simply place two sheets between the white pages and the strip of bookcloth before sewing.

An Oversized Single-Signature Book (C–11)

7. Shallow Boxes

Shallow boxes are made with the outer covering and the inner lining for the sides cut in one piece. This technique is desirable for shallow boxes because seams in the covering material appear only along the edges of the inside of the box.

Determine the measurements of the inside of the box, and cut the base to this size from a piece of cardboard (7–1).

Cut sides W and Y as wide as the width of the cardboard and to the desired height of the box (7–2).

Cut sides X and Z (7–3) to the same height as W and Y, but cut them wider by two cardboard thicknesses than the length of the base. When cut correctly, the box will fit together as shown.

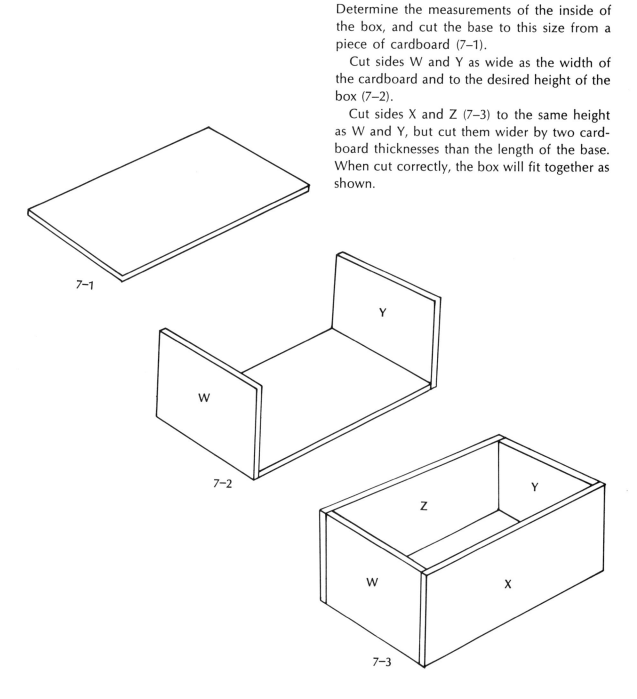

7–1

7–2

7–3

The box is assembled as follows: Brush thick glue along the edges indicated by the solid black lines in 7–4. Let the glue set for a minute to thicken. Position sides W and Y (7–2), then X and Z (7–3). Let the glue dry thoroughly.

To cover the box, cut a piece of paper or bookcloth, with the grain running lengthwise if possible. The covering material should be one inch wider than twice the height of the box and long enough to wrap around the entire outside circumference of the box plus ½" (7–5).

Brush thin glue along the outside of one side of box, X. Position it ½" from the edge as shown (7–5).

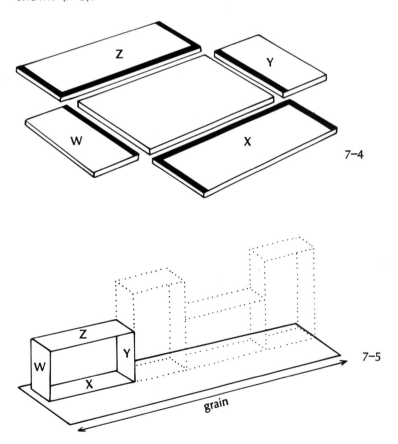

7–4

7–5

grain

70

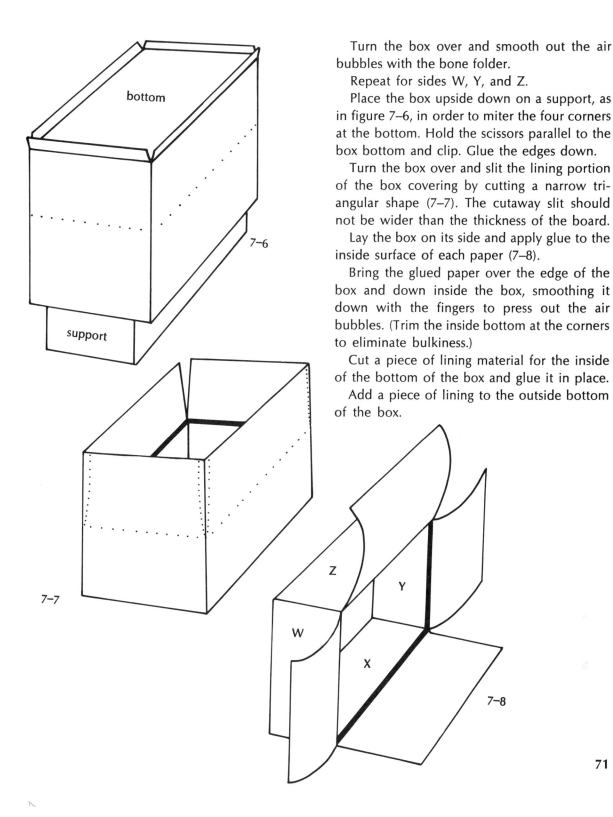

Turn the box over and smooth out the air bubbles with the bone folder.

Repeat for sides W, Y, and Z.

Place the box upside down on a support, as in figure 7–6, in order to miter the four corners at the bottom. Hold the scissors parallel to the box bottom and clip. Glue the edges down.

Turn the box over and slit the lining portion of the box covering by cutting a narrow triangular shape (7–7). The cutaway slit should not be wider than the thickness of the board.

Lay the box on its side and apply glue to the inside surface of each paper (7–8).

Bring the glued paper over the edge of the box and down inside the box, smoothing it down with the fingers to press out the air bubbles. (Trim the inside bottom at the corners to eliminate bulkiness.)

Cut a piece of lining material for the inside of the bottom of the box and glue it in place.

Add a piece of lining to the outside bottom of the box.

bottom

support

7–6

7–7

Z

Y

W

X

7–8

Two Boxes with Covers (7–9)

These covered boxes can be made in a variety of sizes and shapes, following Basic Technique #9. The cover is made like the box; its inner dimensions are the same as the outer dimensions of the box.

A Decorated Box (7–10)

The outer lining piece of the box's cover is a piece of heavy white paper to which a cut-paper design has been glued.

7-9

Two boxes covered with hand-marbled papers.

7-10

The original Polish cutout on this box cover suggests using colored gummed paper to make similar symmetrical designs by cutting on the fold.

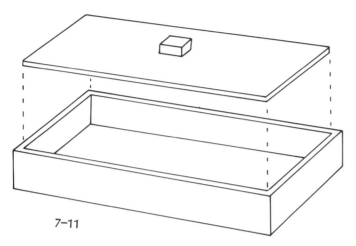

7–11

A Desk Box with Lid (C–12)

This box is made of three or four thicknesses of board. The cover fits inside the box and serves as a paperweight (7–11). It is large enough to accommodate standard-size typing paper. To make the knob, cut six or more small squares of cardboard to the same size, glue together, and cover.

A Picture Frame (7–12)

The bottom of this box is cut to the same size as the picture and the box is built around it as in Basic Technique #9.

7–12

A picture frame holding a starch print.

A Key Holder (7–13)

Make a box to the desired shape.

Cover and line a piece of cardboard with decorative paper to fit snugly in the frame.

To provide space to screw in the key hooks, glue three pieces of corrugated cardboard inside the box before inserting the decorative backing.

Apply adhesive backing to the frame so that it can be attached to the wall (2–17).

A Shallow Box with Hinged Top (7–14)

The cover for this shallow box (made as in 7–12 and 7–13) is made by treating the completed box as if it were a pad, as in Basic Technique #5. The entire outside cover is made out of one piece of bookcloth. A similar cover can be made for any box you already have.

7-13

A key holder covered with bookcloth and Italian decorative paper.

7-14

A single block print repeated would be appropriate on a box of this size.

74

A Large Box (C–13)

This box is covered entirely with bookcloth. The cover is made as in figure 7–14 and covered as in figure 4–15, except that the batik fabric is attached very close to the spine.

A Large Box with Ribbon Ties (7–15)

The box is covered with decorative paper, the cover with bookcloth. Ribbons are attached as in figures 2–10 and 2–11.

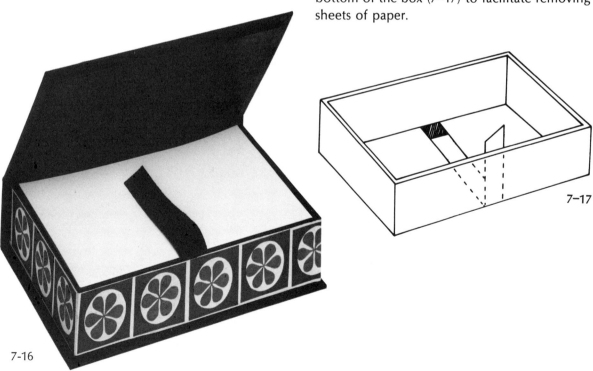

7-15

This large box is covered with English Cockerell paper. The cover is made of bookcloth, with ribbon ties.

A Paper Box with Ribbon Pull (7–16)

A ribbon is glued to the shaded area at the bottom of the box (7–17) to facilitate removing sheets of paper.

7-16

7–17

Paper box with ribbon pull, covered with a block-print decorative paper.

A Box to Hold Unbound Folios (7–18 and 7–19)

A three-sided box is made to fit the size of the folios. Another three-sided box is made to cover the first box. A hinged cover is made slightly larger on each side than the second box (Basic Technique #5) to which the two boxes are glued.

Prepare a three-sided box (7–20) to fit the papers or book which it will contain. (See 7–1, 7–2, and 7–3, but prepare three sides only.) Cover with paper or bookcloth.

Prepare a second box, measuring carefully so that the first box will fit into the second box (7–21). Cover with paper or bookcloth.

Prepare a cover for the two boxes as in Basic Technique #5. The spine of the cover will be $\frac{1}{16}''$ wider than the height of the second box, and each side will be slightly larger than the second box. Cover with decorative paper, bookcloth, or a combination.

Glue the first box on the inside right cover with the open side close to the edge (7–22). Glue the second (larger) box on the inside left cover close to the edge.

Line the spine, pressing the lining well into the grooves.

Line the bottom of each box, using the measurement of the smaller box for both of them.

7-18

This box to hold unbound folios is covered with buckram for The Janus Press.

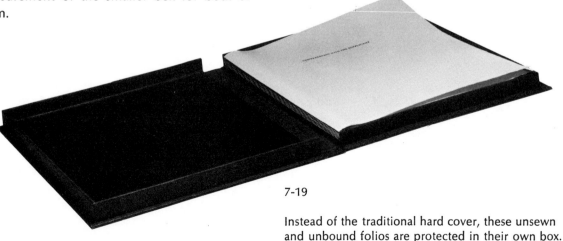

7-19

Instead of the traditional hard cover, these unsewn and unbound folios are protected in their own box.

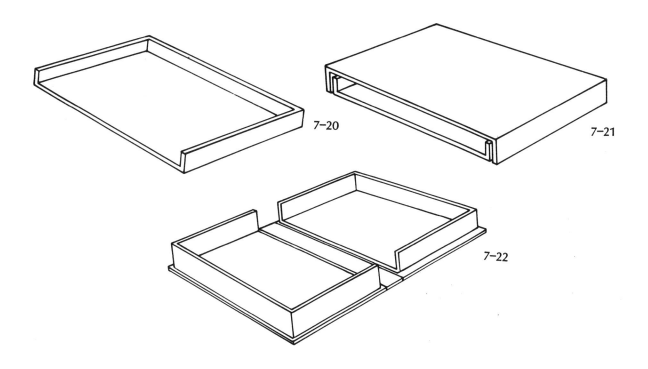

7-20

7-21

7-22

An Open Letter Holder (7–23)

This letter holder is made of cardboard 3″ x 8″ for the base, 4″ x 8″ for the front, and 5″ x 8″ for the back. Four pieces of each are glued together before assembling, in order to obtain the necessary thickness for strength. They are glued as in figure 7–2 with very thick glue and held together with masking tape until dry. Each side is then covered with paper and lined.

7-23

An open letter holder covered with decorative paper.

A Box with a High Shaped Back (7–24)

This type of box could be constructed in a number of ways.

A Letter Holder with Partition (7–25)

This box is shaped and has a divider that is covered with decorative paper and inserted, using thick glue on the edges.

A Small Bookcase (7–26)

This bookcase for holding miniature objects is assembled like a box. Shelves are glued in as in figure 7–24 and are supported by cardboard that is cut to size and glued against the inner side wall.

7-24

This box with a high shaped back is covered with hand-marbled paper.

7-25

This letter holder with partition is made with hand-marbled paper.

78

7-26

A small bookcase covered with Italian decorative paper.

8. Deep Boxes

Because it is difficult to reach inside deep boxes once they are constructed, they cannot be easily made with the covering and lining cut in one piece as shown in the previous chapter.

It is not necessary to line a deep box, but if it is lined, this should be done before the sides are glued together. The lining may contrast with the outer covering or match it. A seam will appear inside the box where the lining and the outer covering meet, but this seam is not visible in a tall box.

Line a piece of cardboard on both sides before cutting. If the cardboard becomes too warped for accurate construction, let the glue dry until the board becomes flat.

Cut the pieces for the box as in Basic Technique #9.

Assemble the box with the lining facing the inside.

Cut a piece of decorative material long enough to wrap around the box plus ¼″ overlap and about ¾″ wider than the height of the box.

Apply glue to the paper and roll the box up in it (8–1).

Miter the paper edges at the bottom of the box (7–6) and glue them down.

Slit the paper edges at the top of the box (8–2) and glue them to the inside of the box. Press down well with the bone folder.

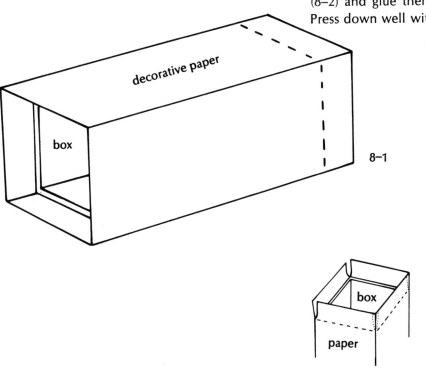

8–1

8–2

A Tall Pencil Box (8–3)
Pencils are covered as in 2–14.

A Mini-Pencil Bin and Matching Pad (C–14)
Golf pencils, available at stationery stores, can be covered with any color paper.

A Box Holding Score Pads and Pencils (8–4)
A pencil box, partially covered with bookcloth, has a panel of decorative paper glued to the completed box. Pencils are covered to match. The box is built around the size of the four purchased score pads and pencils.

8-3

A potato print on paper covers this pencil bin and matching pencils.

8-4

A bin holding score pads and pencils, both covered with Italian decorative paper.

82

A Four-part Pencil Holder (C–15)

Four pencil bins are glued together before being covered. Thin cardboard, cut to size, is glued over each side to cover the line where the boxes met. The box is then covered as in 8–2, and paper is added to the top.

A Napkin Holder (8–5)

An Open Paper Box (8–6)

8-5

A napkin holder covered with decorative paper.

8-6

This open paper box is covered with decorative paper.

A Tall Box with Cover (8–7)

This box is constructed of many thicknesses of board. The cover has a knob also made of many thicknesses of cardboard. Several pieces of board are glued together, covered, and added to the inside of the cover to hold it in place on the box (8–8).

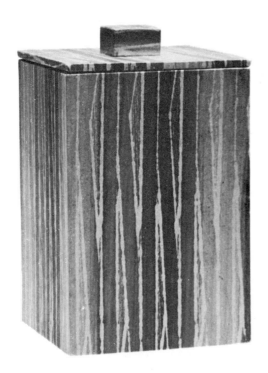

8-7

This box is covered with Swedish paper batik.

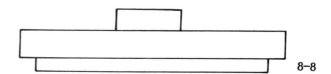

8–8

A Slipcase for a Narrow Book (C–16)

The board is lined before being cut to fit the dimensions of the small album it will contain. The box is constructed as if it were a tall box as in Basic Technique #10.

A Slipcase for Four Books (C–17)

Several thicknesses of board, the height and combined width of the four books to be contained in the slipcase, are glued together (8–9). The thickness of the board is determined by the depth of the abacus that is to be inserted in the wall.

An opening is made the size of a tiny purchased abacus, so that it can be forced in.

The sides are lined and added around the base board (the board that has the opening). This base, too, is covered with an additional lined board. The height of the sides is equal to the depth of the books resting on this board (8–10).

The abacus is forced into the opening after the box is covered with bookcloth. A decorative border is added to match the color of the abacus.

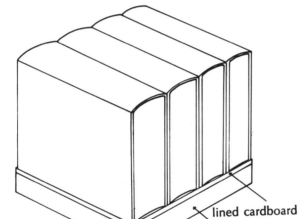

lined cardboard

8–9

cardboard with opening

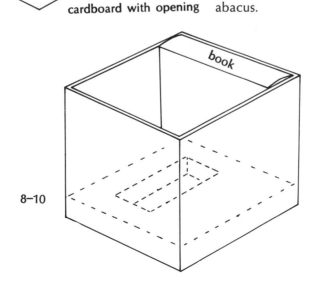

book

8–10

A Small Chest of Drawers (8–11)

Construct a box 5″ x 2½″ x 5″ in a shape to hold three drawers.

Cover the box with decorative paper as in Basic Technique #10.

Measure and cut dividers or shelves on which the drawers will rest.

Apply glue to the edges and insert, holding in place until the shelves adhere.

Construct three drawers as in figure 7–3. Before adding the lining to the bottom of the drawers, glue ribbon pulls in place.

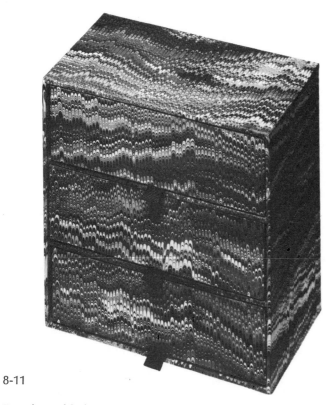

8-11

French marbled paper covers this small chest of drawers.

8-12

This box was constructed to fit the design from a Christmas card. The box is covered with a small design to complement the charming linoleum print by Ellen Egger.

A Box with Cover and Inside Panels (8–12)

Starting with two bases of the same dimensions, build a box and a cover as shown in figure 8–13. Cover them with decorative paper using Basic Technique #9 for the top of the box and Basic Technique #10 for the bottom. Line the inside and outside bottoms of both boxes.

Cut pieces of thin cardboard so that they are about ⅛″ narrower than each side of the box and ½″ higher when resting on the bottom of the box (8–14).

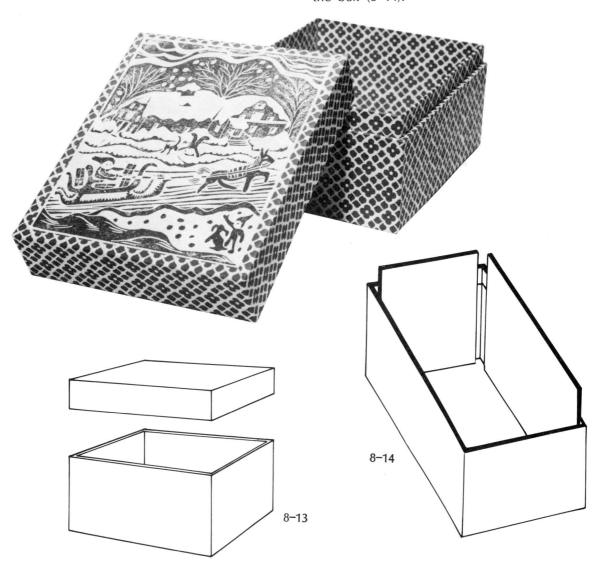

8–13

8–14

Cut a piece of decorative paper $\frac{1}{2}''$ wider than the height of the panels and long enough so that the panels can fit on one edge of the paper, as shown in 8–15, leaving $\frac{1}{16}''$ between each panel and adding $\frac{1}{2}''$ at the end. Glue the panels to the decorative paper.

Turn down the edge of the paper (8–16).

Bring the two end panels together, having the decorative paper on the inside. Press them together to make them stick (8–17).

Brush glue on the inside walls of the bottom of the box and insert these additional panels. Use clothespins to hold the sides together until they adhere.

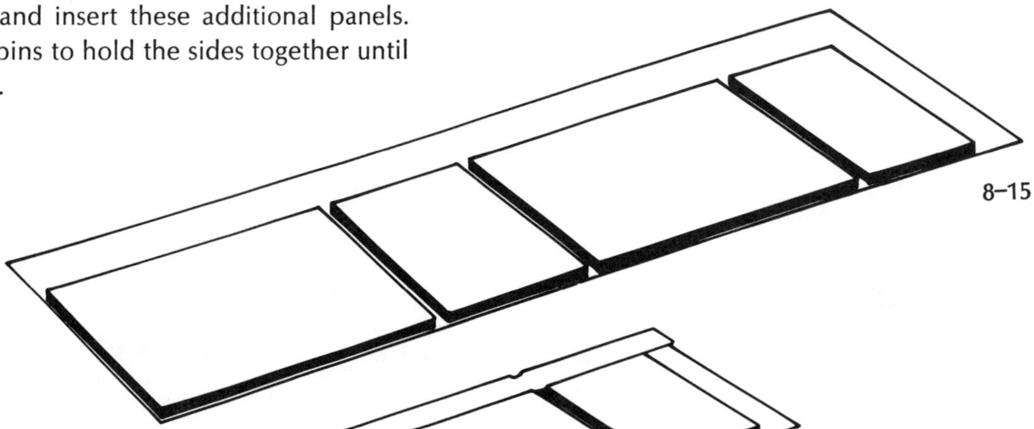

8–15

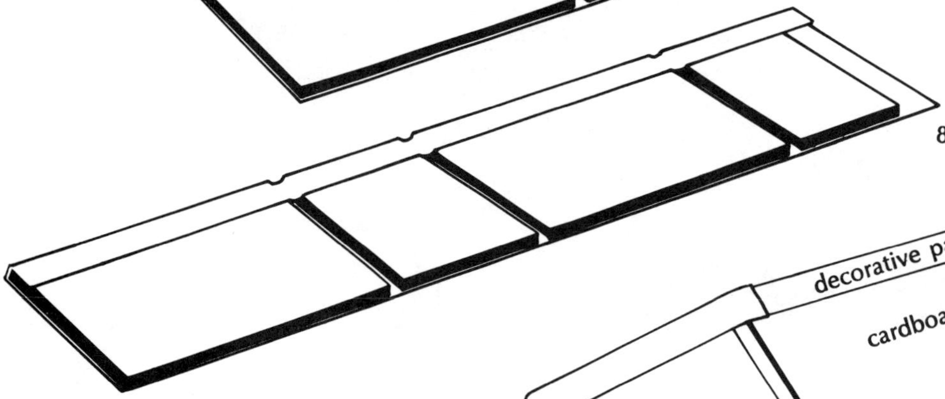

8–16

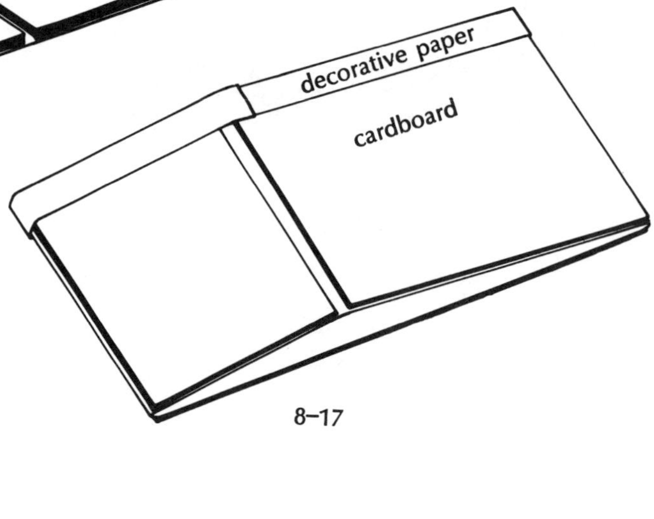

decorative paper

cardboard

8–17

A File Box Covered with Paper (8–18)

A box of this type is made as shown in figure 8–12. However, care should be taken to make the measurements of the inside wall large enough to hold the standard-size cards used.

The cover is hinged to the back of the box with a piece of bookcloth. Decorative paper conceals the hinge and covers the entire back.

A File Box Covered with Fabric (8–19)

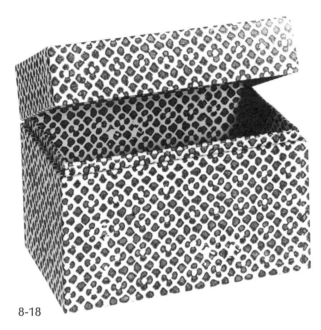

8-18

A file box covered with decorative paper.

8-19

This file box is covered with an India print cotton fabric that did not require a paper lining.

A Box with Tray (8–20)

This box has a raised tray held in place with covered cardboard supports (8–21). The cover is made like a note pad cover (Basic Technique #5).

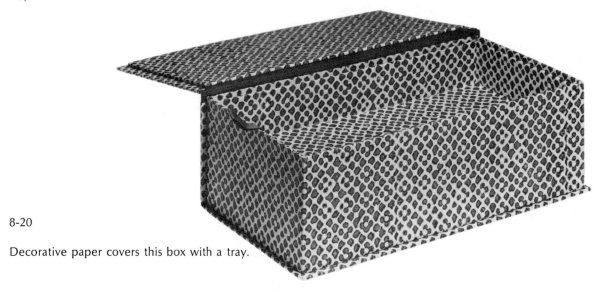

8-20

Decorative paper covers this box with a tray.

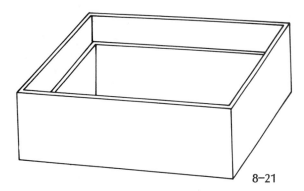

8–21

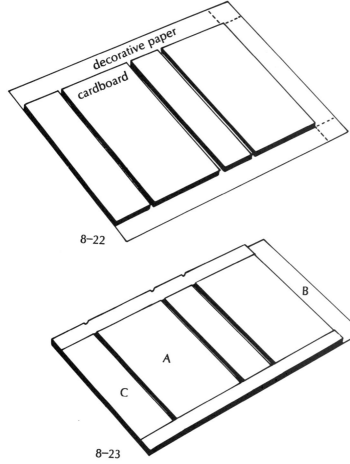

8–22

8–23

A Matchbox (C–18)

Construct a box to hold kitchen matches. Cover with decorative paper.

Cut four strips of cardboard the length of the box. Two of them should be slightly wider than the height of the box and the other two should be slightly wider than the width of the box.

The boards should be glued to the decorative paper as in figure 8–22, leaving $\frac{1}{16}''$ between the boards and $\frac{5}{8}''$ extra on the three sides as shown. Trim away the corners on the dotted lines. Fold down the two long sides (8–23), boning down well. Line the entire inside with bookcloth.

Place the matchbox face down on A and bring the hinged parts around it, gluing B to the right side of C. Cover the seam with striking material cut from a commercial match box.

A Wallboard (C–19)

Cover and line a large board of several thicknesses.

Glue to it various sizes of covered boxes, pads, and paperclips to hold all your needs. Or, make smaller boards—all different.

Further Reading

Brown, Margaret R., and Etherington, Don. *Boxes for the Protection of Rare Books: Their Design and Construction*. Washington, D.C.: Library of Congress, 1982.

An outstanding and copiously illustrated looseleaf publication with detailed instructions. (Available from the Superintendent of Documents, U.S. Government Printing Office, Washington, D.C. 20402-1575.)

Cockerell, Douglas. *Bookbinding and the Care of Books*. New York: Taplinger Publishing Co., Pentalic Books, 1978.

A paperback reprint of a classic originally published in 1901 and revised several times.

Diehl, Edith. *Bookbinding: Its Background and Technique*. 2 vols. 1946. Reprint (2 vols. in 1). New York: Dover Publications, 1980.

The definitive work on hand bookbinding in English.

Grünebaum, Gabriele. *How to Marbleize Paper: Step-by-Step Instructions for 12 Traditional Patterns*. New York: Dover Publications, 1984.

An easy-to-follow illustrated guide to the entire marbleizing process.

Hollander, Annette. *Cover a Book to Look Like a Million*. New York: Fawcett Publications, 1970.

A pamphlet with instructions for making book covers and decorative papers.

————. "Cover a Book to Look Like a Million." *Woman's Day Magazine*, February 1970.

Includes color photographs of decorative book coverings.

————. *Decorative Papers and Fabrics*. New York: Van Nostrand Reinhold Co., 1971.

Instructions for the techniques of marbling, fold-and-dye papers, wax-resist and potato printing, and starch-paper prints. (Out of print, but still available from Bookcraft, P.O. Box 6048, Hamden, CT 06517.)

————. "Fold Dye Papers." *Woman's Day Magazine*, September 1970.

Instructions for fold-and-dye papers, with color photographs.

Hunter, Dard. *Papermaking: The History and Technique of an Ancient Craft*. 2d ed. 1947. Reprint. New York: Dover Publications, 1978.

This is *the* work on papermaking in English.

Johnson, Pauline. *Creative Bookbinding*. Seattle: University of Washington Press, 1973.

Simple binding techniques for the amateur.

Kafka, Francis J. *Batik, Tie Dyeing, Stenciling, Silk Screen, Block Printing: The Hand Decoration of Fabrics*. 1959. Reprint. New York: Dover Publications, 1973.

Step-by-step explanations with illustrations to guide you through each technique.

———. *How to Clothbind a Paperback Book: A Step-by-Step Guide for Beginners*. New York: Dover Publications, 1980.

Simple and inexpensive method of binding.

Lewis, Arthur W. *Basic Bookbinding*. 1952. Reprint. New York: Dover Publications, 1957.

Simple enough for the beginner yet still of interest to the expert.

Roberts, Matt T., and Etherington, Don. *Bookbinding and the Conservation of Books: A Dictionary of Descriptive Terminology*. Washington, D.C.: Library of Congress, 1982.

An excellent reference. (Available from the Superintendent of Documents, U.S. Government Printing Office, Washington, D.C. 20402-1575.)

Saurman, Judith B., and Pierce, Judith A. *Ready-to-Use Marbleized Papers: 12 Full-Color 11½" × 18" Sheets for Craft Projects*. New York: Dover Publications, 1979.

Attractive, inexpensive and ready to use.

Notes on the Cover Illustrations

C–1   Desk-Blotter Holder with Vertical Panels (page 29). Gift-wrap paper is used to cover this desk-blotter holder. Bookcloth or paper-lined fabric could be used for the side panels.

C–2   Large Photo Album (page 33). This photo album is covered with fabric. (Batik design by Anne Feidelson.)

C–3   Photo Album with Plastic Sleeves (page 47). This photo album with plastic sleeve panels is covered with fabric. (Batik design by Evelyn R. Warner.)

C–4   Fabric Paperback Book Cover (page 52). (Batik design by Anne Feidelson.)

C–5   Telephone-Directory Cover (page 52). This telephone directory is covered with fabric and bookcloth. (Batik design by Anne Feidelson.)

C–6   Letter Portfolio (page 54). Wallpaper is used to decorate this double-pocket letter portfolio. The inside is lined with bookcloth.

C–7   Three-Panel Writing Portfolio (page 54). This portfolio is covered with fabric and bookcloth. (Batik design by Anne Feidelson.)

C–8   Portfolio to Hold Drawings (page 55). This large portfolio for holding drawings is covered with fabric. The design was made by dipping corks in wax and printing on the fabric. After several dye baths, the wax was ironed off. (Design by Anne Feidelson.)

C–9   Letter Portfolio (page 57). Natural finish buckram bookcloth and a tiny wallpaper print are used to cover this letter portfolio.

C–10   Cloth-Covered Book (page 65). Jersey fabric was laminated to paper prior to being applied to the cover of this blank-paged book.

C–11   Oversized Single-Signature Book (page 67). This 10″ × 16″ hand-sewn single-signature book is covered with a fold-and-dye design on rice paper.

C–12   Desk Box with Lid (page 73). This desk box with cover is decorated with hand-printed paper.

C–13   Large Box (page 75). This box, measuring 13″ × 15″ × 3″, is covered with bookcloth. The lid is decorated with a hand-made batik fabric. (Batik design by Anne Feidelson.)

C–14 Mini-Pencil Bin and Matching Pad (page 82). Gift-wrap paper is used to decorate this matching box and pad. The pad is constructed by stapling paper together and gluing the outer sheets to the inside of the cover. Golf pencils are covered with paper to match.

C–15 Four-part Pencil Holder (page 83). Hand-marbled paper is used to cover this pencil bin.

C–16 Slipcase for a Narrow Book (page 85). This slipcase is covered with bookcloth and the book it holds is covered with fabric. (Batik design by Anne Feidelson.)

C–17 Slipcase for Four Books (page 85). This slipcase containing a small abacus was made to hold four books on mathematics. It is covered with bookcloth and trimmed with paper. (Designed and executed by William V. Hollander.)

C–18 Matchbox (page 91). This matchbox is covered with hand-marbled paper.

C–19 Wallboard (page 91). Boxes covered with various hand-printed papers were attached to this paper-covered wallboard.